TETHERED

A NOVELLA-IN-FLASH

ROSS JEFFERY

PRAISE FOR TETHERED

'From boyhood to manhood, Ross Jeffery's Tethered mines the trappings and tragedies of modern masculinity. This innovative novella-in flash will punch you in the heart when you aren't looking. It hurts, but it feels so good too.'

Michael Graves - Author of Dirty One and Parade

"*Tethered* uses the form of flash fiction to create bursts of a father-son relationship seen from both sides, about the ties that bind, often painfully, about the damages inflicted and inherited, handed on, and how the cycle can be broken, the punches finally pulled."

Lucy Caldwell - Author of Intimacies and Multitudes

'Ross Jeffery's flash fiction is immediate, visceral and real. To read his stories is to feel the understanding of a life lived through the eyes of a compassionate man. Always unapologetic, always raw, always true.'

Adam Lock - Author of Dinosaur

'Ultimately Tethered is a short, intense portrait of a troubled father-son relationship and an examination of the 'strange labyrinth' of parenting.'

Roisín O'Donnell - Author of Wild Quiet

'Tethered tells the story of a difficult relationship and Jeffery writes movingly and unflinchingly about the push and pull of love between a father and son. I read this in one sitting, immersed, traumatised and impressed by this searingly honest portrayal of power and tragedy born of a desire to be better. I loved it.'

Hannah Persaud - Author of The Codes of Love

'With effective use of the novella-in-flash form, Ross Jeffery tackles a challenging subject with unflinching honesty.'

Diane Simmons - Author of Finding a Way

"In the immortal words of Philip Larkin: 'They f*ck you up, your mum and dad / They may not mean to, but they do.' Ross Jeffery takes these words to heart as he deftly paints a beautiful, and painful, portrait of a troubled father-and-son relationship. Searingly honest and insightful, to the point of feeling confessional, *Tethered* will lead you towards its heartbreaking and emotionally devastating conclusion with the authority of parent's hand."

Joseph Sale - Author of The Black Gate Trilogy

––––––––––

''Tethered' the novella in flash by Ross Jeffery, is a touching and sometimes shocking story about the violence and tenderness in a father/son relationship over one life time. In vivid, urgent prose, Jeffery gives insights into a man's struggle to become a good father in this society, where emotions are still seen as weak, strength is valued over vulnerability, but where love and forgiveness win over in the end. Read this novella and learn from it.'

Jude Higgins - Author of *The Chemist's House*

––––––––––

'A searing indictment of toxic masculinity'

Karen Jones - Author of The Upside-Down Jesus and Other Stories

––––––––––

'*Tethered* is a visceral reflection on father and son relationships. At once sharp like a punch in the face and as warm and comforting as being lifted by a giant from the back seat of a Ford Sierra when pretending to be asleep. Ross Jeffery's prose is immediate and at times arresting in its observations. There were moments I laughed out loud, cringed, gritted my teeth and wanted to cry. If the mark of good art is to make us feel, then *Tethered* does it with a bright, challenging intensity.'

Dan Soule - Author of *Neolithica*

For Dad,
my very own Superman

CONTENTS

DADHOOD

There's something very special about being a dad and when you're blessed with a son? Wow. An overwhelming sense of joy that eclipses that of a daughter - the family name will live on.

Selfish I know, but there's something very biblical about it. My name will carry on long after I'm rotting in the ground.

With a son there's so much more you can do with them than with a daughter – rough and tumbling on the floor, teaching them to fight, shooting stuff with toy bows and arrows, and when they're older, maybe even shotguns and clay pigeons. His first tool box and first football match, cowboys and Indians, teaching him how to build stuff and how to take it apart, and most importantly how to fix things around the house. I love my daughter, but she doesn't get me, not like my son will.

. . .

Or is it that I don't get her? I wasn't made that way. You see, I was hardcoded to make and break stuff with my hands. I wasn't built to play with dolls or role-play mummies and daddies. I need some escapism from the mundane chores of parenthood. And the boy, he'll be my way out of painting nails, playing dolls, dressing-up and tea parties.

He'll be a mini me; I'll teach him what I could never teach a daughter.

I glance down at his little head, nestled in the crook of my elbow, my hand holding onto his tiny bottom, legs hanging down either side: skinny with tiny socks on the ends like cotton buds.

The wife's sleeping. It was a long and drawn out labour, but he's here now; my little guy. Perfect in every way. He's got my scowl already, I watch him wriggle in my arm, feel something loosen in his nappy, it's probably wind, but in that moment he looks just like me. I can tell he's going to be a fighter, a determined little sod that'll test me at times, but he'll always be the apple of my eye, I'm sure a bit of tough love will see him straight. Never did me any harm.

My father was never around much, even before he decided to not be around at all. My mum, she was too ill to look after us, sent away to some godforsaken asylum to rot, poor mare. So Dad was on his own - didn't take long for him to give me and my brother up to an orphanage. Not because he *couldn't* cope, mind you. He just chose not to bother trying. Moved in with Mrs. Tibbet next door and had new kids with her. Charming, hey? We were just little... how could he forget about us so freely? So easily?

'I'll never, ever give up on you son,' I whisper in front of the window, rocking you side-to-side as we glance out over the world he'll go on to conquer. *'Just don't grow up to be one of those queers...'* I whisper as I stroke his nose *'...one queen in this country is more than enough.'* I tug your hat down, cover the pulsating web of flesh, hide it from view. He begins to stir, uncoordinated arms flap around. I slide my finger down his nose, gently rub it, soothe him back to sleep. One slip... violence is always so close, isn't it?

Unforgivable. Those people that hurt children. There's a hot place in hell for those sick bastards – how could you? Why would you? Sick. That's what they are, fucking sick monsters. If someone ever hurt my boy like that, I wouldn't know what I'd do, I'd probably kill them, cut their fucking dicks off, and I'd go to prison for it; go to prison for him. I'd die before I let something like that happen to my boy.

When I lose it, I fucking lose it. Sick bastards.

I put my finger in his open palm, his tiny fingers close around it. Purplish nails gleaming in the light, each finger perfectly formed, miniature, fragile. I can't help but think of all the things he'll do with those hands: of what this little bag of bones will become and do with his life. Whatever he does, I'll be proud and I'll tell him often; my dad wasn't there for me, but I'll always be there for him, through it all, through the ups and downs: I'll be as dependable to him as gravity. Always there to cheer him on and a force to ground him when he needs it, just in case he starts getting ideas above his station. No one likes a precocious little brat.

As he clutches my finger I try to remember this moment, this time right here is the most unspoilt he'll ever be, the world will chew him up and spit him out; but here, now, he's like the virgin snow, clean and perfect. I know all too well that this world makes grey slush of peoples' lives, a sudden thaw leaving everything bare and exposed and in the open, however hard we try to hide our disappointments, mistakes and hurt.

But for now he's perfect and I'll try and keep him that way. *'I'd die for you little man. Do you hear me? I'd die for you!'* I feel his little hand squeeze harder at my words. A bond forged right there and then; I tilt him up, show him the world outside the window: full of all the shit this world will sling at him.

I've no idea on how to be a dad, how to raise a son. This job doesn't come with an instruction manual which is probably why so many people fuck it up. I just hope *I* don't fuck it up. But can it *really* be all that difficult?

ON THE SHOULDERS OF GIANTS

Up here on my father's shoulders the air smells crisp, even his cigarette smoke takes on a sweet and comforting odour, instead of the choking blanket that awaits me down there.

Up here I can see what's coming, whereas down there I have no idea: things lurk, things pounce, and things have a way of creeping up on me.

Up here I feel safe, but down there I feel vulnerable.

Up here I can escape, down there I'm a prisoner.

Up here I feel special, as if I'm on a throne, being shown off to the world, but down there I feel I'm hidden, pushed about and forgotten.

. . .

Up here I feel cherished, but down there I feel like discarded rubbish.

Up here the world is full of life and light, down there it's suffocating and dark: ominous and shadow clad.

Up here I can fly; I put my arms out and glide, whereas down there I'm grounded, my wings clipped.

Up here I feel I belong, down there I'm lost.

Up here I encounter the fullness of Winters, Springs, Summers and Autumns, but down there, only failures and disappointments.

Up here I can sing, shout and laugh, but down there I sob, cry and wail.

Up here I avoid capture, but down there I am overcome.

Up here I am at peace, but all awaits me down there is war.

Up here there is love, down there is only sorrow.

. . .

Up here anything is possible, but down there it's all too much.

Up here there is colour, but down there it's colourless.

Up here I believe, whereas down there I doubt.

Up here is peace but down there only shouts, arguments and rage.

Up here the bruises look like dappled shadows landing on her skin, but down there they are just bruises: brownish yellow and green, the colour of Autumn leaves.

Up here I grow sad, because I know that shortly I have to return to down there.

3

BONK

'Right, sit there and don't move.' I place the boy on the kitchen worktop. His wailing persists. Tears streaming, nose running, a slug trail leading to his mouth: he tongues at the ebbing current like a lizard.

'Listen. Stop. Stop your crying, you sound like some sissy boy!' He flinches at my raised voice.

'You want to grow up big and strong like your Daddy, right?' He nods. Eyes wide with fear.

'Then what you need to do is stop this bloody crying. You don't see Daddy crying when he hurts himself, do you? You didn't see me crying when I did this?' Lifting my hand I wave my latest injury before him, a sand-belt accident, and half my index finger gone in an instant. A fleshy raw stump remains, pink with new flesh. I point it at him, well, half point: he shifts his gaze.

'Listen boy, never, I mean *never* let anyone see you cry, it makes you look weak and pathetic...now suck it up!' He stops wailing, lip quivering, betraying his inner turmoil. He's desperate to please me, he always is; but I can see he's going to be weak, just like his mother.

Bending down I tug at his Ninja Turtle sock. He's got odd ones on. I pull the Leonardo one off. Drop it on the floor. Michelangelo stares at me, waving his nunchucks from the other foot. Why his sister threw a brick at a spider, I'll never know. Her aim's shit, throws like a goddamn girl: something to work on later I suppose.

I grab his leg: he winces, the bruise big and bulbous on his ankle, blood pooling under his youthful skin, a brick pattern emerging as though he's been branded. His lip quivers as I prod it, test the joint for a break. All fine. He cries silent tears which patter on his shorts as they drop from his face.

'You know what we need to do right?' he stares at me, vacant, fearful. 'We need to do a bonk.'

'What's a bonk?' he offers through ragged breaths. Sniffs up a yellowy slug escaping his nose.

· · ·

'Well, a bonk is what you do when you hurt yourself. Someone gives you a bonk and it's all better.'

He sits there. I open the freezer. Red or blue? I take both, slip them in my back pocket. Turn back to the boy.

'I think I'd like a bonk, what's it like, will it hurt?' he says.

'Well, it's like this.' I step towards him. Lift my hand towards his face. It's huge against his tiny head. I forget how young he still is. My fingers, like a gorilla's in girth and roughness, twist into a fist; I allow my short digit to stick out like a nub, as if I'm going to knock on a door. I rap him on the nose lightly.

'Bonk.' I say. He blinks at the tap.

He sits there contemplative, makes eye contact 'It feels better, Daddy!', a smile breaks out.

'See, told you it works. So anytime you hurt yourself again, we'll give you a bonk, there's no need to cry about it...okay?' he nods.

'Right... red or blue?'

.   .   .

He ponders as a four-year-old does, most difficult question he'll be asked today.

'Red.' He shouts, giddy with excitement.

'Good choice!' I pull the ice-pole from my pocket. Cut the end, hand it over. He sticks it straight in his mouth. Sucks. Pacified.

I pull the blue one from my pocket, crush it in my hands, mould it around his ankle; he winces as I press it on, but firms up fast, that's my boy.

'Good boy!' I say.

4

DRESSES AND DRAGS

I once wore a dress. A beautiful polka dot number: navy with huge white spots. The bodice of the dress had been tight against my chest, I remember liking how it felt, how I was secure within its silky embrace: like a never-ending hug from my mum. At the waist it puffed out with various pleats. It had a netted petticoat underneath, that rubbed against my legs: I wasn't a fan of that, but my sister said it didn't come off, so I had to learn to love it.

When I span around in front of the mirror, the pleats fanned out and the dress rose, like an upside-down tulip opening its petals. My slim legs, busy spinning me around beneath its billowing canopy. I'd never felt more free and happy than I did in that moment. I'd giggled with joy, unable to contain it. When I'd sat down I watched how it slowly settled around me, hiding my folded legs beneath it. I remember how I stroked the fabric, felt how soft it was. Awed at how pretty it was. *Boys clothes are never this special,* I'd thought; made for running, jumping, climbing: things I enjoyed. But this, this felt extraordinary.

My sister had knelt beside me. Pulled out her bag of nail polishes. Grabbed my hand from the dress, pulled it toward her; placed it on her knee. She picked up a bottle of polish: red like a million melted rubies. Struggled with the lid for a time and then I heard it crack open. I love my sister, but she doesn't play with me as much as I'd like, she'll only do it if I submit to her games first. This was one of her games. I wouldn't admit it to her, but I kind of enjoy this time together, being made to look pretty for once.

I let her paint my nails. I watched as she delicately dipped the brush into the polish, her tongue sticking out at the side of her mouth, which it does when she's concentrating. She moved the brush three times on each nail. One long blob down the middle, then one stroke on either side. She'd move onto the next nail. Kept on going until all the nails on that hand were painted. She told me to blow them, taking my other hand in hers and starting the process again.

I gently blew at my fingers; smelled the paint as I waved them back and forth in front of my mouth. My hand looked delicate, like a china doll's. I wished I could have them painted all the time, but my sister said '*boys don't usually have their nails painted, they'll call you names at school*'. I held up my hand and splayed my fingers, '*boys can be so mean,*' I'd thought. My sister had just nodded and carried on painting my other hand.

· · ·

When she'd finished, she put the polish in her bag, tucked it back under her bed. I sat there waving my hands, blowing on them. My sister had put some music on; asked me to dance. We danced like crazy in our dresses. She left me; said she needed the toilet. I didn't mind I was having the time of my life, spinning around and around watching the dress rise and fall with my spinning. Dizzy with excitement, I left the room in search of her, joy flowed around me, billowed out of me like my dress as I left the room and looked for her. She was in the lounge: I could hear cartoons on the television; she'd lied. She'd gone off to do her own thing, again.

I marched in to get her, to ask her if she'd play my game now.

'What in hell are you wearing?', my dad had spat at me. I stood there. In my dress. Knees trembling. I put my hands behind my back quickly, hoped that he wouldn't see my nails. He'd got up from his seat, strode across the room. Grabbed at the dress, almost lifted me off my feet. I heard the fabric tear within his vice-like grasp. I'd glanced at the shoulder: it was torn. I felt myself getting hot; a rage burned within me, tears welled up from somewhere deep within me.

'I'm... I'm...' I couldn't get the words out. *I'm wearing a dress,* I wanted to say, but it was stuck down inside my throat and wouldn't come out.

'No son of mine will ever be caught dead in a dress. Take it off. Now!' I stood there. Tears flowed. I lifted my hand to rub them away. He snatched at it. Held my wrist. Shook it. 'What the hell is this?', as he held my hand up to my face.

'Nail... nail polish.' Never in all my life had I dared to speak so freely.

He laughed a bloodthirsty cackle 'Nail polish. What the hell are you playing at, you want to be a bloody sissy. Is that it? You want to dress up like a woman? Not in my bloody house you won't. Now get in there and take it off!'. He shoved me out the room, marched me to the bedroom and aggressively pulled the dress off in a frenzied scuffle. I heard it rip. Watched as it was left tattered and torn on the floor. He didn't care. He just loved destroying things that were beautiful.

Afterward he scrubbed at my nails with paint thinner, my fingers stung with the harshness of the chemicals. He told me to *keep quiet,* that *I only had myself to blame*; although it hurt, it was more distressing seeing my nails return to normal. Joy stripped away with each furious swipe.

That night I got the slipper; and I never put a dress on again.

5

SPOONING

A father's worst fear is not being able to help their child, believe me I know. But I tried, I did. He just wouldn't listen: takes after his stubborn mother.

I warned him not to eat all the grapes, but did he listen to me? No, no he fucking didn't.

Scoffed them down like a fat kid does cake: and now I'm paying the price for his stupidity.

Time off work.

Delay to the groundworks.

. . .

The cranes.

The bricklayers.

He doesn't even care: why would he? To him everything in this world revolves around him. Doesn't have a scooby-fuck-ing-doo about the ways of the world. That his decision to eat two punnets of grapes affects more than just his bowels. *It affects people's livelihoods,* I'd shouted at him.

Told him he was selfish, berated him until he cried. Dumb kid. Sitting there on the toilet bound up and red faced: sweating, hyperventilating as he tried to squeeze out a shit. Crying and dribbling, face a runny mess. Sobbing for his mother. Such a mummy's boy when things get tough; I need to teach him that that don't get you much in life: being a sissy. Teach him that you can only rely on yourself when the shit hits the fan. How much I wish it would, because now we're here at the hospital and he's still not taken a dump.

He reaches out a hand. He's on all fours. The doctors move around behind him. He's in a gown but his arse is on show to the world and their mother. His little clammy hand rests on mine. I feel it tremble like the wings of a moth fluttering over my knuckles. He grabs hold of my thumb at the same time a doctor grabs at his hips: manoeuvring him into the right position.

. . .

In this moment it's like I see him for the first time in years. My throat contracts, I feel a swelling in my heart. I don't like this feeling, I try to choke it down but it keeps rising like bile in my throat, I'm unable to smother it. The thoughts come thick and fast, heavy and claustrophobic.

He's just a little boy.

He's worried.

He needs me.

For the first time in a long while I can be there for him. Concern of what's about to happen carves his face up into a distended grimace; brown eyes like chocolate discs stare up at me engraved with fear.

I clasp his tiny hands in mine: lost within my huge swaddling digits. I lean forwards; smell his sweet breath laced with a breakfast of Coco Pops, toast and strawberry jam. He looks scared. I go to talk and he flinches away. Worried about what I'm about to say or do. It strikes me hard like the fizz of a cattle prod, bright, light and painful. He's about to endure something terrible, but he doesn't fear it, what he fears is me.

. . .

'It's okay son, it'll all be fine.' a smile breaks out across his face: it seems awkward, an expression he seems to have forgotten how to do in front of me. 'You okay?' I shake his hand lightly. He nods. Sniffs. Pulls my hands closer.

The doctors are busying themselves out of view. Metal instruments clang around us as they're placed on the tray behind him. Clinical.

'Dad?' his small voice almost lost in the din of the room.

I glance down. His eyes, big and petrified, unblinking and scared - pleading.

'What is it son?' My voice feels fragile, alien, like at any moment it'll fracture into a thousand pieces. I watch as he weighs up his response.

'I'm scared... is it going to hurt?' he mumbles.

'I'm sure it'll all be fine, they do this all the time.' I don't make eye contact; I can't lie to him, not again, not so soon. 'Just try to relax.' I lift my other hand and bonk him on the nose with my finger. Our little code, what we do when he hurts himself - he offers a small smirk of appreciation but his eyes betray his inner turmoil.

. . .

His hand's clasped tightly over mine now. He grips my thumb, I feel it going numb. With each of the doctor's manoeuvres, he winces, flinches. I stare over his raised back at the doctors, masked and gloved as they use what looks like a silver spoon to dig out his backed-up excrement. They're so blasé about it: as if they're just digging hardened chocolate ice-cream from a tub. Each scoop, each insertion into my son's bum bringing more of the dank, nutty looking and putrid smelling shit into the room - where it's dumped into a mound on a tray. Each time the spoon goes in his arse my son bucks, squeezes my hand, sobs. He's scared, stares at me, non-verbally pleading me to make it stop, but he knows not to ask me to make them.

After about twenty minutes the ritual digging stops. The doctor tells us that it's all over. We sit there in silence as they wheel away the trolley and the shit and leave us in the room alone. The silence is deafening. I can tell he's upset, that he feels violated. Ashamed. I pick up the prescription for the laxatives they'd left us. Tap the box within the paper bag in my hands. The boy pulls on his Spiderman pants, then his trousers, slips his shoes on and we head for the door.

I watch him waddle ahead of me. He gets to the door and turns around. His face riddled with inner turmoil, something he doesn't know how to voice; he stares at the floor as if after what's happened, what I've witnessed, he couldn't look me in the eye: as if I'd see him differently now.

. . .

I need to make this right. I need him to know I care, that I'm always for him and not against him.

'Hey... son?' He glances up, eyes pooling with water.

'Yeah?'

'You want to get some ice cream?' He runs at me, arms outstretched almost knocking me off my feet as he hugs me.

'Yes please, Dad!'

RAINING GOLF BALLS

'Y ou paralysed streak of piss!' Dad yells from the driver's seat. Headlights bearing down on us from behind. The car lurches. I flounder in the backseat. Petrified. Mute.

Headlights swerve to the left.

'No you fucking don't!' he hisses, pulls at the steering wheel. Dragging us back in front of the beam. The headlights reflect blindingly from the rear-view mirror, demon eyes staring at me. My hand reaches out for my sister's: dances over the backseat. It finds nothing because she's not there. She's with my mother, and how I wish I was too.

'This'll learn'ya...' He sneers. Left hand reaching for the glovebox. The car lurches to the side. The juddering of crossing cats-eyes in the road. His head darts to his mirrors, quickly he pulls us back in front of the car behind. Snaps the glovebox closed, drops his find into his lap.

Flashing lights now. Each flash reveals a more menacing, grotesque face staring at me, through me, at his intended target: behind. He lifts his hand. His fingers fumbling with some white ball. It's one of our golf balls. The ones I found in the park. Unmarred. *I love Dad,* I'd written on it.

He said he'd keep it forever.

Dad twirls it in his hand like some sadistic David Bowie, from that film Labyrinth. Full-beam highlights grow large behind.

'Right, you bastard, how'd you like these apples!'

Dad unlatches the sunroof. Drops *our* golf ball out. It disappears. Clanks on the roof. Bounces off the boot. A light blinks out behind. One remains. Dad laughs as honking erupts from behind; doesn't see me crying. Grabs a fistful more, each one special, each one a memory. Stuffs them through the sunroof. They sound like hail hammering down on us. Tinkling. Bouncing. The other light goes out. There's a screech. A bang. Silence.

TOUGH CHOICES

A nticipation was in the air. It always is on Saturday mornings, my time with the boy.

He dressed quickly, throwing his clothes on. Only now, his sweaty hand in mine, do I realise his t-shirt's on backwards and inside out. I take a drag on my cigarette.

We look left, right, left again, before we can even think of crossing. Since doing the Green Cross Code at school, he's become a stickler for the rules.

It's spitting; we wait for an appropriate gap in the traffic, heads flitting side-to-side as if we're watching tennis. She's watching us from above the cobblers shop, from our window. I tug the boys arm. Nod towards her. He glances up to the window. A smile cracks across his face, we both wave at his mother as we wait to cross.

He's distracted, still looking up: so I yank him across the road, dodge a 208 bus and make it to the other side. His mother would pander to his Green Cross bull-shit, I won't. Safely on the other side he runs off; splashing in puddles as he goes, I flick my cigarette into the gutter as we reach the newsagent's.

Door swings open, bells chime our arrival. The boy runs into the Aladdin's cave before us. Sanjay nods from the counter.

'Good morning sir, what will he pick today?'

'Not sure, you had another delivery?'

'Yes...yesterday. I'm sure he'll find something?'

'Sure he will, I'll grab twenty B&H on the way out.'

'I'll keep them here ready, I know you'll be a while!'

The smell of old curries and joss sticks is thick and sickly; I raise my arm, sniff my donkey jacket, the smell already permeating my clothes. I turn the corner. His tiny frame dwarfed by the huge carousel; little fingers already roving through the figures, a method to his quest. He whips the carousel around, working his way up in a corkscrew motion.

'Got... got... got... don't got... ooooooo... really want!' Holds a box in his hands, pawing over it, turns it over. Glances up at me, sheepish; I nod to the floor. He places Yoda down and keeps searching.

'No way... they got a Jawa, with the vinyl cape and everything! Dad look, a Jawa!' I hear Sanjay chuckle from behind his counter. Turn. Sanjay lifts two thumbs up; sure he would, because he's not the one buying one of these damned things. Overpriced pieces of crap, here today and gone tomorrow; they won't last. Why doesn't he want a tool box or something practical?

Turn back to the boy. He's put it on the floor, joining the growing pile of plastic and cardboard at his feet. Pulls another from the carousel; 'Hammerhead', this one's called. Drops it to the floor, hands already reaching for another one.

'This one looks like you Daddy!' I shuffle forwards, peer at the name. 'Yak Face'. He's a joker.

. . .

'Right, which one do you want?'

'One?' He glances down, the pile at his feet. He's broken I can tell, but I'm not made of money. The boy drops to his knees. Smears the plastic with his clammy hands, fingers dancing over each box; heart-breaking but money doesn't grow on trees, you're never too young to learn that lesson.

He separates the boxes, a discard pile including 'Yak Face' and something called an 'Ewok', and a keep pile, with the 'Jawa', 'Boba Fett' and 'Yoda'.

'Right just pick one!' I shout. He fusses about on the floor. I wander off down the aisles, grab a paper and head back to the boy.

He's sobbing now, a mess on the floor. I bend down, level with his face. Put a hand on his shoulder, he shrinks away, as if I'm some kind of monster. Holds two out to me, I take them. Yoda and the Jawa. Eyes two iridescent pools of water, I wait for them to burst, they don't. I hold a toy in each hand. His lip quivers.

'Which one?' I utter calmly.

'I... don't... know...' he stutters back.

.   .   .

'Pick one, or they'll both go back.'

He points, hand shaking, 'Jawa' wins. Tears roll down his face, quickly he wipes them away with the cuff of his jumper. He knows what I think of him crying, I've had to tell him enough. We put the remaining toys on the carousel. He skulks off, waits at the door.

Sanjay rings it through the till; the toy, paper, my twenty B&H.

'Is that all today sir?'

'One minute...' I turn, head back to the carousel. The boy's still staring out the window. I come back to the counter, hand Sanjay 'Yoda'.

'Put the B&H back, I'll get this one too...' a smirk breaks out on Sanjay's face. I pay. Tuck the toy under my jumper, take the plastic bag.

'Same time next week?' Sanjay proffers.

I smile back; nod, then steer the boy out of the shop by the back of his head.

· · ·

Huddled under the bus stop, the rain still falling, heavier now; he's sad, I can tell. He kicks a discarded can into the gutter. I hand him the 'Jawa'. His face lights up, eyes widen, he pulls it in close, hugs it. I kneel down opposite him; feel the wetness of the ground seeping into my jeans.

'Do you like it?' he silently contemplates my question, goes to say something but stops, his lip quivering again.

'Well, what do you think of this one?' I reach under my jumper, pull out 'Yoda'. His face blossoms into a gaping, gap-toothed smile. He runs the short distance to me, flings arms around my neck. I put a hand on his back, feel his heart racing.

'Thank you Dad!' his breath light and warm at my neck.

'Can I keep both?' he whispers.

'Of course you can, my special little boy!'

I never want to forget this feeling.

UNCLE

(ORIGINALLY PUBLISHED IN ELEPHANTS NEVER)

The carpet's rough. Its bristly nibs bite into my skin. Can't breathe, my father splayed out on top of me: his full weight baring down, choking the oxygen from my lungs. Muscles burn, cramp throttles my calf like a snake coiling around a tree trunk. But still he pushes me to the carpet. Sweat covers us. We are two slick eels, a couple of greased up Greco wrestlers.

He presses his club-sized hand down against the side of my head. The stench of sawdust and Bensons and Hedges, his rough hands, like sandpaper, set about rubbing away: robbing me of my youth, forever powerless, eternally put in my place. I can feel his short index finger worming its way into my ear. He'd lost it to a sanding belt accident: the stub; both grotesque and mesmerising all at once.

He dips his head lower as I flail. Can't rid myself of his ballast. His breath at my neck, the heat of his panting, the noisome reek of roast dinner stuck between his teeth and the sour, musty smell of beer. His body loosens; a chance to escape. I move but his powerful body springs into action, slamming me back into the carpet, a million bristles stabbing. Submission. We've a safe word. But I don't dare utter it. This time will be different. I'm sure of it.

His hands all over me: grabbing my wrists, holding my legs down, pressing my face against the floor, subduing my efforts at escape with ease: a thousand-armed tormentor. Finally, he straddles me. I let him. His huge hands splay out across my shoulders, pinning me down. He leans in again. Dragging with him the oniony ripe notes of body odour.

'Say it...' he utters. The safe word, he means.

I try to wriggle free again, but it's pointless: there's nothing I can do. His hand lets go of my shoulder, grabs the back of my neck. Don't know how long I've tried to fight it. I feel weak. I'm a boy and he's a man. A sapling crushed beneath a mighty oak tree; what am I meant to do?

'Tell me...' he says, his breathing ragged.

He's lying on top of me. I'm cloaked in a menacing shadow. He grabs one of my wrists, it burns.

. . .

'Say it!' he snarls. Breaks into a mocking laugh.

I surrender. Let it happen.

'Uncle,' I say. 'Uncle... I give up!'

9

LIFE IN THE DIRT

I take the measurements.

Buy the wood.

Sort the tools.

Calm the boy.

Shout at him for his continued crying, for being silly, for being such a girl about things.

He goes off to his room, slams the door, opens it and apologises for slamming it; closes it again.

. . .

I set to work at the dining room table. Draw the measurements on the wood and place the pencil down. With the ruler I go back to the mound of kitchen roll on the table, a small lump hidden within. I pull it open revealing his hamster.

It was blind and in pain, so death was probably a sweet release for it. Its eyes had hardened into crusts over its face: yellowy scabs with a black centre. I'd asked the boy what had happened and he said that he loved her so much that he just wanted to squeeze her, hug her; well he did that all right. Squeezed the living shit out of it. Since then it had been stumbling around its cage blind and in pain for a week; but we don't have pet insurance (*as it's a waste of good money*) so it had to suffer, boy needs to learn that things live and things die and between those two things you suffer, you grin and you bare it and sometimes you survive it. I wasn't just going to throw my hard earned money at prolonging the inevitable. Its hobbling came to an end this morning.

The boy ran in to our bedroom, woke me up, his face slick with tears and snot. 'Snowy... she's... she's... dead!' he uttered, his breathing ragged like he was having another asthma attack. I stumbled down the hall after him, found him kneeling in front of the cage, a sorry bloody sight. As I came in I could see it lying there, in the corner of its cage. No signs of life. I reached in, lifted it from the sawdust floor, it had been dead for a long time, rigor mortis had set in. Its little paws together in a silent prayer.

. . .

I double-check the measurements of the body, fold the tissue over and turn back to the wood. Within a half hour I've something vaguely resembling a wooden box, I'm a builder so making a coffin for a pet is a piece of piss. But it's still half an hour I'm never getting back. It pains me seeing how emotional he gets; he's just like his mother: needs to grow a spine, be a bloody man for once in his life.

I fetch some cotton wool. Fill the box with it. Then call for the boy. I hear him jump down from his bunk bed, trundle to the door. Then hear his feet on the stairs: sniffing all the way down. He comes to the table, red eyes, puffy face; he's been crying for hours. He slips into the chair next to me, silent. He notices the little coffin. I see his face shift, a small smile beginning to break through his sombre exterior. 'Go on then, pop her in!' I say, maybe a bit too jovially, but I'm done: this has taken up far too much of my time already. He sniffs, rubs at his leaking nose, reaches out a trembling hand to the kitchen roll. He starts sobbing again, tears streaming down his face.

Then suddenly, like a slap in the face, I see him like it's the first time. I see the pain he's gained from what he has lost and it's all too familiar. My god. The deep well of sadness so familiar to me, so inherently part of my person that I have since stopped noticing its presence, rises like an overflowing sewer so that all of a sudden, I smell its pungent ugly odour and I know it's too close. I don't want it here, the aching chasm, where my childhood should have been. Where *my* dad should have been. I did go to his funeral in the end. Felt it was my duty. Burying that man's body was just an act of formality though. Put my own dad in the ground and did it without feeling a thing. That's what being an orphan can do to you. A childhood filled with feeling rejected and unloveable teaches you that feelings are nothing but dispensable luxuries. Too busy trying to survive instead. But I can shield my boy from that. If I can just shield him from any unnecessary pain: if I can take it away, I'll save him the heartache. A small mercy, for now at least. Some things a boy shouldn't have to do and burying something you love is one of those things.

I still his hand, pull it towards me. His little hands trembling within mine as he glances up through tears, sees my eyes getting wet too. I reach out and pull him into me, where he sobs. Unsure of his surroundings he goes rigid, not sure if I'm going to ridicule him or comfort him, if my tears are of anger for his weakness. 'It's okay son... I'll do it, you shouldn't have to, you shouldn't have to... I'll take care of it.'

I lift the body of the hamster and place it within the box, all the while the boy just watches his arms folded on the table and his head resting, tilted to the side on top of them. I ask the boy if he wants to put some food in there, in case she gets hungry. He nods. I grab a handful of sunflower seeds and scatter them inside. I pick up the lid and place it over her. Slowly I pick up the nails and begin to seal it shut.

Once sealed, I slide the box over to my son, it's heavier than

I imagined. He picks up a pen and scrawls a message of love on the top of the box, slides it back – '*I'll always remember you Snowy x*'. It breaks my heart how sensitive he is, but reminds me how I can learn from him, that although I think I have it all figured out, there's so much more I need to learn. I pick the box up and hold out my hand to him. He takes it, and we head out to the garden, where I've already dug a hole to put the coffin in and made a tiny cross. As we step out into the frigid air he squeezes my hand. I look down at him and he sniffs before breaking my heart again.

'Sorry dad... for being upset.' I stop dead in my tracks, crouch down look him in his big swollen eyes.

'Son, you've nothing to be sorry for. I should be the one to be saying sorry.' I rub the tears from his cheek and we head towards the grave hand in hand, father and son.

DROWNING FOR DRACHMA

W hen I was little, I died. Almost.

Ever since I was old enough to walk, I'd had a predilection to be in water: the bath at home, the stream in the woods, the Mediterranean, a puddle in Downham - if it had water in it I'd be there.

'You'll be the death of me! You're staying under too long!', I recall Dad bellowing, as my head finally pops out of the water, like an otter coming to the surface to check its surroundings.

Don't get me wrong, I could swim on top of the water, no problem at all. But I preferred it beneath, where I could disappear; it was different down there: I belonged.

. . .

Dad would sip his Amstel, tossing coins into the water as if he was feeding the ducks. With stinging eyes and burning throat, I'd dive to the bottom of the pool, fetch up the coins.

I'd break the surface, coins ready for the next round.

'Wonder you ain't some type of fish,' my father would say.

I was eager to please him; always was, but especially then, because after the game, if I'd done a good job, I'd get to keep the coins.

'Got more front than Blackpool, my boy!' he'd say to everyone and no-one all at once. Desperate for someone to acknowledge his wit, while I wondered why my attention and adoration wasn't enough for him.

To me he'll always be a sea urchin: sharp, prickly, someone who needs to be handled with care, his temper vehement.

I came up with a fistful of drachma and all of a sudden felt a foot connect with my face. A cloud of bubbles erupted from my mouth. There is no time for me to reach for more air as I am forced under the water, again and again. Through flashes of shape and colour, I can see it's another boy, about my age. For a moment I think he's doing it on purpose: holding me down, clawing, pushing me deeper, but I hear wails that aren't mine and I realise he is using me as a life preserver, as he struggles to keep his head above the water. I go under again. It was glassy down there, everything moved slowly; I struggled to rise, but was pushed further down. Towards the forgotten coins at the bottom of the pool, dancing within the fractured prisms of light.

An eclipse soon blocked everything out. Two hands burst into the water; I recognised those hands: the roughness, the shortened index finger. They hauled me from the depths, a coughing, spluttering mess, where I sat, curled, secure and nestled in his tanned leathery arms. He nursed me and I let him.

I was his boy and he was my urchin, a son and a father. I let him pierce me with his spikes, deflating into his arms like a punctured beach ball.

HUMP DAY

The dog was a gift for the boy. I didn't want it but somehow I left the place with it. Skinny little mutt, spindly legs, shaggy coat, in need of fattening up; its little eyes stared out through a mop of long scraggy hair; quaking like it had taken one too many beatings. I felt sorry for the little thing, but it strangely reminded me of the boy: that's why I got it.

Since we buried his hamster, he'd felt lost. Moping around the house all weekend. Like he has anything to be sulking about? The boy doesn't even know he's born half the time, doesn't know how lucky he is at his age. Wait 'til the world chews him up and spits him out, then he'll have something to look sorry for.

I half-walk, half-drag the stinking mutt back to our flat. Pull at his leash, hear it yelp: but soon he just walks on without cocking his bloody leg every few steps, leaking urine all over the pavement. That's why I didn't want to get a bloody dog, because who's going to be the sorry bastard taking it for walks all the time, yeah that's right it's going to be me. As if I don't already have enough to do.

The wife says it'll help, we can go out on family walks, go to the woods, enjoy some time outdoors. That sounds great in the summer, but in the winter when it's pissing down, pitch black and ice on the ground; what then? I can already bloody tell you, she ain't gunna be the one getting out of bed at the crack of dawn, dragging this sorry sack of shit around the park: it'll be me.

I take the mangey looking thing up to the flat. Open the door and he stands there shaking at the threshold. It's then I hope that this skinny little thing is housetrained. I forgot to ask. I do enough bloody tidying up in this place with two ungrateful children, all their toys and shit in every room. My days of cleaning up shit are well and truly behind me – there is no way we're returning to that.

I realise we don't have any food for the dog, so I open a can of beans: drop it into a cereal bowl and leave it on the kitchen floor. The wife will be home soon with the boy and his sister. I'm actually quite excited to see his little face when he sees his new pal. Relief more than anything, give him something to be happy about, so I don't have to watch his sad little face whilst I'm eating my dinner.

· · ·

The dog wanders towards the lounge, his feet padding and nails clacking on the hallway floor before he steps gingerly onto the carpet. It walks over to my feet and lies down. Rests its head on my foot. Whimpers slightly, unsure of its surroundings: I reach down and stroke his fur. His head flits back and licks my hand.

The door opens and the cacophony of two children home from school fills the house: a herd of fucking elephants. I'm normally not here when they get home and I realise now why that is. I always stop off at the pub for a sly beer before coming back to this madhouse. The dog's quivering at my feet: shaking, unsure.

The boy comes running down the hall, throwing his schoolbag to the floor with a loud thump, turns into the lounge. Stops dead in his tracks when he sees me, shocked that I'm home, he takes a step back. Then he sees the dog. His eyes brighten, his face unfurls from a frown into a smile – the first genuine smile I've seen in a while.

'Go on.' I say, nudge the dog to move. It bounds across the carpet, starts sniffing at the boy, its tail wagging. It spins around at his feet, sits, then stands. It doesn't know what to do; it turns and bounds back into the room, the boy moves after it. It jumps up at him, two front paws resting on his chest; he holds them, spins with him, the dog hopping around with him on its back legs, licking the boy's face.

They move together: a strange ballet taking place in the lounge. He's never been happier.

Later on in the evening, the boy's playing with his toys, crouched over on the floor. Dog forgotten as I knew it would be. It slinks in and out of the rooms in the flat, smelling the doorframes. I've already stopped it pissing a thousand times and taken it for three walks on the flat roof outside. It wanders back into the lounge, sees the boy on the floor and runs at him, jumping on his back, tries to ride him. The boy turns around, stands up and the dogs at him again. All too late I realise what's happening. The boy doesn't, why would he? Then I see the dog grabbing my sons leg, the dogs back arched, paws clasped around my sons leg and its hips start thrusting.

'Daddy he's dancing with me! Look! He's really dancing!' the boy shouts out in a spate of giggles. I get up from my seat, the dog still humping away, the boy continues dancing with it – oblivious to what's really happening.

I kick the dog. It whimpers then bares its teeth at me with a snarl, its lips quivering. I move the boy behind me as it eyes him up. It barks, snaps at us. I herd it out of the room, back towards the kitchen. Each time it turns back, snarling, teeth white and bright in its black gums.

The dog had to go. It was violent and there was no place for violence in our house, that's what I told the boy. He eyed me suspiciously, like he wanted to say something, but kept his mouth shut. Tears trickled down his face: he sniffed, nodded his head.

'I understand.' He spluttered, composed himself 'Thanks Dad', sniffed again. 'I've never danced with a dog before, it was nice whilst it lasted!'.

BANISTERS AND VOLCANOES

I hear them screaming. Her at him. Him at her.

Dad slams a fist hard onto the table - glasses and cutlery rattle into the uproar unfolding downstairs.

I sit, unmoving at the top of the stairs. Hands grip the banisters: knuckles turn the colour of bone. Scared.

Press my face against the wooden balustrade: eyes search. Find only shadows. The argument plays out on the wall, a zoetrope: flickers of rage projected in shifting candlelight.

Dad screams. Guttural rage erupts into the night; the

volcano blows its stack. We'll be buried in his hot ash for days, if not weeks. His feet stomp around the dining room, floorboards groan their displeasure. Dad kicks at a chair. It slams to the floor. The cat hurtles up the stairs, disappears into my room.

Mum pleads. Sobs. Dad continues thrashing around. His rage a crawling lava, spreads. Ensnares everything in its path: corrupts, destroys, wilts any hope before it has a chance to be born.

A whimper. My sister. Huddled next to me. Drawn to the sound, like eyes to a car crash. We sit, hear the volcanic tremors below. Things snap, break, clang about. A gold chain tinkles to the floor, is kicked to the bottom of the stairs. My mother's. She weeps. Sniffs. Collects her necklace. I ease back out of view. Peer through the banisters.

Sister hugs her knees, which are inside her long '*My Little Pony*' nightie. She's older than me, but when things like this happen, she sucks on her thumb: index finger rubbing at her nose. She rocks slowly, back and forth. Like those orphans we saw in the news, in Romania. Ghost children.

'I'm gunna kill that fucking bastard!' Dad yells. I shrink back. Sister descends further into her nightie. Eyes big. Wet. Peer out, frightened. A glass smashes on the wall. We flinch.

. . .

'No...no...don't do it,' Mum screams. Shadows pull at each other on the wall '...don't....don't...'

They tear apart. One lands heavily on the floor. Dad's shadow stands tall, ominous. He flees to the door, feet stamp, sound his escape. Door creeks open. Slams with a thud that makes the panes of glass rattle.

'...don't go!' Mum's exhausted cries fall on deaf ears. Dad never hears it. Car starts, tyres screech. Mum alone, broken, weeps.

I stand. My sister pulls at my top, not wanting me to leave her. Another hand grips mine: clammy and feverish, it urges me to stay; so I do stay and I hold her hand, squeeze it tight. I never want to let it go. She's scared. I'm shaking uncontrollably, pulling in ragged breaths. With legs like jelly I stand.

'I have to go', I tell my sister, with a facial gesture and head nod. She loosens her grip, one clammy finger at a time, releasing me as I drift off. Float towards the stairs. Towards the ash heap and chaos below - my own Pompeii awaits. I need to be brave, I tell myself. I need to be strong, for my sister and my mother but it feels like a stiff breeze would knock me right over.

I take a first faltering step. Want to turn back, pretend it all didn't happen. But I can't. I can't put this back in the box. I realise with a blinding clarity that I've got to do it, I've got to be the man of the house. So I take another step.

WHEN AN UNSTOPPABLE FORCE MEETS GRISTLE AND FLESH

F lecks drop to the floor. Discarded like wood shavings.

Jeans dirty, shirt bloody, hands shaking. Can't stop them. Adrenaline leaving the body. For the first time, I'm scared. Alone. A single tear escapes.

The bed's hard. Solid concrete. Thin mattress, even thinner sheet. Glance down. Feet. Says Tuesday on my sock, but I know it's Friday. A hole in the left toe. A pink worm inside. I wriggle it to check. Just a toe.

Turn my hands over. Blood. Dried the colour of rust. Rub at my stubble, head throbbing. Touch the ragged wound above my right eye. Lightning strikes my brain.

. . .

'Stupid bastard deserved it. No one takes me for a ride. Showed him who the fucking boss was didn't I? Treated that sack of shit to a front row seat.'

His nose gave way easily. A bloody eruption. Crunch of gristle, like biting a ripe and juicy grape. Crack. But his children, their faces. Haunted. As I felled their Superman with my kryptonite skull, like a dead tree.

I hear their screaming. Coming back to me in waves. His wife weeping, a record stuck on repeat. Sobbing over that tightfisted sack of shit squirming on the floor. All he had to do was pay me what he owed.

His nose spread out across his face. Me the sculptor. His face wet clay, as I set about rearranging it with vengeance and spite.

I fled with blood trickling down my face. His. Mine. Mingling together. Nowhere to go but here.

'We're in a quandary,' they said.

Apparently, no one ever hands themselves in. Said I might be experiencing shock or shame, a mixture of both.

. . .

'We'll put you in here for a few hours.' They said.

'See if anyone comes forward, to press charges. Give you time to think about things.'

My thoughts swallow me like a tsunami.

I'm not shocked at what I've done. I meant to do it. Shame? I don't even know what that's like, never felt it, never had to. I might be? Sure. But I won't let anyone see it. Wife. Daughter. Son. They'll never see it. I'll bury it. Deep inside. I'll always be right. Even when I'm wrong.

CUTTING LABELS FROM KNICKERS

T he beetle was on its back trying to right itself. Big and blackish purple. Like a bruise. Size of my thumb nail. I'd been watching it since I came up here. Sunlight slashed across the white tiled floor. Sat with my back against the sun-bleached door. Flecks of peeling paint rough against my back.

The cold tiles hurt to sit on. Swimming shorts damp, uncomfortable, in the sudden cool of the hotel corridor. If I believed my dad, which I don't, I'd get piles. He didn't tell me what they were, mind you. He just said, 'Don't go sitting on cold surfaces, you'll get piles!' When he told me, it reminded me of when we'd got home after walking in the snow last winter. Cold. Sodden feet. My sister and I pushed the soles of our feet against the radiator. Felt the warmth seep through my skin, thawing frozen toes, watched them turn from white to pink.

· · ·

He shouted: 'Get your feet off there, you'll get chilblains!' and rushed into the room as if saving us from a fire, batting our feet from the radiator. But he never told us what they were either; I doubt he even knows. But we were scared all the same.

The beetle spun in an arch, floundering. I felt its pain. Stranded and lost. Wanting someone to play with it, help it. I knocked on the door again.

I could hear grunting, heavy breathing from inside: a soft lilt of appreciation at the end of each painful groan. But still no answer. The netting in my shorts was chafing. I checked to see no one was watching, slipped a hand inside and shuffled my bits and pieces around. Cold and shrivelled. My hand froze, scared I'd find something other than my balls or dick — maybe one of those pile things. I freed the netting and reclined in the heat in sweet relief.

Crouching down. Shimmying across the floor on my stomach, like a caught fish in the belly of a boat, I wriggled closer. The beetle was still moving. Movements slowing, it was giving up. Heat and exhaustion. I flicked at it. It span on the spot. I flicked again with an upward arch. It flew up into the air, rolled over a few times, then landed on its legs. It was still for a moment, then scuttled away.

I knocked again. 'Mum?' nothing but a whimper from behind the door. 'Dad?' I knocked louder.

. . .

'What the fuck now?' Dad's hushed voice talking to my mother.

I heard his feet pad to the door. It opened a crack. Dad appeared and glanced down at where I was sat. He was breathing heavily, a sheen of sweat across his face and torso. His lower half covered with a towel.

'What?' he spat between deep breaths.

'Are you coming to play?'

'I said I'd be down in a minute...'

'But it's been fifteen!'

'Go and play with your sister.' He turned back into the room, door opening a little. The bed was messy. His clothes on the floor like stepping stones towards the bed. I could see mum's leg, tanned and slick. Her foot hanging off the end. Her knickers twisted like a pretzel on the floor. I craned my neck, peering inside. She was wrapped in a sheet, naked. Dad saw me. He pulled the door towards him and spoke through the crack.

. . .

'Mummy and Daddy are busy.' Sweat trickled down his torso, disappearing into the towel.

'W...w... why's Mummy naked?' I stuttered.

'I'm just helping Mummy with something...'

'What?'

'I'm just... helping her. Cutting the labels out of her knickers... she said they were hurting her... anyway you're going to catch your death waiting there for me. Go back to the pool and play with your sister and I'll be there in a bit! Okay?'

He didn't wait for a reply. The door closed. Feet padded away. Bed groaned. Hushed voices. Laughter. Moans.

I waited but didn't want to catch my death. I plodded my way back to the pool, path hot under my feet. I ran. I didn't want to catch chilblains either.

The label in my swimming shorts cuts into my back, each stride making it worse. Maybe I'll ask Dad to cut it out later too, he seems to really enjoy it.

15

WRESTLING

I push him down onto the carpet. Press my body up against him, I go limp and subdue his movements. 'Get out of that without moving', I whisper in his ear. His body goes limp, lost beneath my bulk. I lift myself, stare at his face. He's play acting. Waiting for me to shift my weight for him to scramble free and try to mount me. I lift off him slightly and wait. Then he springs into action, his sapling like arms reach out and grab hold of my thick oak-like leg. He flounders beneath me. Fury burning within his eyes at being made to feel small, yet again, in front of his watching mother and sister.

But he is small. I'm the Alpha and he's the Beta. There's only one outcome.

He's bitten off more than he can chew this time. He flails, trying to spin around and looks up at me, trying to find a way out of the tangle of limbs. He's panting, his eyes wide with what looks like hate: it could be embarrassment, possibly disdain for me, but I've broad shoulders so can carry his disappointment in me. I push him down harder this time, my hand on his chest, pinning him beneath my iron sized hand. I feel his ribs beneath my fingers, housing his beating, throbbing, racing heart. He's going red: angry at being subdued so easily, made to look like a little boy; again. But he needs to learn that he can't always win. I always win. The sooner he realises that he's lost, the better. It'll serve him well in life to know that he can't always get his own way, no matter how much he thrashes or spits or screams. It builds character, this thrashing and subsequent defeat: therapy, almost; it never did me any harm. Like gorillas in the forest: the silverback always wins, always knocks the young upstart back down to size, and harmony is restored. He knows this. When will he learn?

His two dainty hands reach around my thumb and little finger. He uses all his strength to lift my hand from his chest, bending my fingers backwards. I see his wafer like arms struggling and relent a little, make him feel like he's gaining the upper-hand as he bench-presses my hand from his chest slowly. I won't give him the satisfaction of doing it with ease. His arms wobble with the exertion. Like a jack about to succumb to the pressure of a car too heavy for it. I let him lift it off, give him the sense of accomplishment. His face brightens with the thought of escape; that he might have won. But then I quickly straddle him across his waist, pinning him yet again; hope dying in his face, as I show him that his thrashing is useless, that there is no escape. I will win, as I always do, and he will lose.

· · ·

His skin's covered in red rashes, welts and scratches as our movements become more erratic, frenzied almost: limbs flying back and forth like two cats rolling around trying to gain an advantage. I lift an arm too quickly, my elbow cracking off something soft and wet. He goes limp. I sit up straddling him still. See the fear in his eyes. The Despair. The Failure. The Hate.

Watch his eyes well up with tears. They escape down the side of his face, pour into ears then run over and disappear into his sweat covered hair. His lip quivers. His mother shouts at me 'get off him': it sounds distant and far off. 'Can't you see you've gone too far this time?' the bewailing of a protective mother. Then I see his lip quiver. Swelling. Blood trickling from the corner of his mouth. I feel his body shake beneath me, trembling like a beaten dog, I slide off him. But he remains still, frozen. I reach out to touch him. He flinches away. Suddenly he scampers to his feet and flees, to the safety of his bedroom, away from me.

I hurt him.

I never meant to hurt him.

It was just a game.

16

THE BOSS

My Dad said he hated his boss but I think he had an odd way of showing it.

Every Saturday morning he'd come into the lounge wearing his dressing gown and announce '*I'm spending some time with the boss*'. I'd be eating my porridge in front of the television and he'd work his way over to his record player. A Bensons and Hedges hanging from between his thin lips, under his wiry moustache.

He'd lift the plastic cover off the record player. Pull the same record sleeve out from the shelf. Tilt the sleeve up, reach inside and pull out the vinyl record. Placing the cardboard container on the shelf, he'd turn the record over in his thick hands. I'd never seen him treat anything so delicately, it was as if he was scared of it, not even my mother was treated so softly.

. . .

He'd lift the black shiny disk into the morning light. Bring it up to his eyes and stare at it, the smoke from his cigarette would creep up his face and into his eyes, he'd pinch one eye shut like Popeye and carry on observing its surface. The cigarette dancing within his pinched mouth. I'd catch a glimpse of the vinyl, it looked like a black tree stump. All the rings swirling around, each one catching the light. My uncle said that when you cut a tree open you can see how old it is by the rings. I guess Dad was seeing if the vinyl had aged over the week.

He'd blow it a few times. Sometimes he'd try and pick some dust off it with his fingers, he'd always start with his hand that had a shorter index finger, the one he lost to a sand belt accident. Then he'd change it up and use his hand with all the bits and pieces of his fingers still in place.

Sometimes he'd turn to me and say, '*you been touching it again*'. An accusation rather than a question '*There's greasy little fingers all over the bloody thing*'. I'd deny it. Shake my head. Pretend my mouth was full of food so I couldn't answer and he'd be able to tell I was lying, because I *had* been touching it, of course I had. I wanted to see why he wanted to spend so much time with his boss but I wasn't going to tell him that, I'd get the slipper for sure.

He'd pick up a rag that he stored on top of the records. He'd swirl it around the surface. Working his way from the middle to the outer edge. Then he'd snap the cloth away from the record and I'd see all the dust fly into the air, mingling with his cigarette smoke. He'd place the record on the turntable, chuck the cloth back to its resting place, then stub out his cigarette in the ashtray on the coffee table before leaving the room.

I'd always have enough time to finish my porridge and then pick up his stubbed-out cigarette. I'd place it between my lips and for a moment, pretend to be my dad and I realise that that is all I really want: to be just like him. The cigarette always tasted disgusting and it was always a little moist on the end: the taste would stay on my lips for hours. I'd quickly put it back in the ashtray when I heard him creaking back down the stairs.

He'd come into the lounge wearing his blue jeans with the little red rectangle on the back-right pocket and a white t-shirt; his battered red baseball cap on his head. He'd have his leather belt on, which I'd felt a few times when I'd been caught doing something naughty. It had this metal buckle on it that when it caught you, you knew you were in for some hurt – but there was something about that belt that made me want to own it. Who knows, maybe one day I will.

Dad would just stand there, opposite the record player. Waiting. Breathing.

. . .

He'd reach out and pick up his headphones, slip the grey plastic things with yellowish foam on the ends over his head and onto his ears. The foam was rough, it felt like the sponge that mum used on me in the bath when I'd get all muddy and she'd have to scrub my elbows and knees.

He'd plug the long wire that was attached to them into the record player. Then he'd reach over to the sideboard, grab another cigarette. He'd roll his Zippo lighter down his leg and up again and magically the flame would be there to light his cigarette. He was so cool. He'd lean forwards and click the arm of the record player and it would slowly lower onto the slick surface of the record as it began to spin.

I'd watch on as my dad was lost to his routine.

He hated his boss with a passion. But he always seemed to enjoy this special time with him.

Just him and the boss. Dancing. Smoking. Singing.

I quite liked my dad's boss – he seemed to have a calming influence on him, seemed to transform him into someone we'd rarely see: so care free and happy. He'd sometimes hold out his hand to me. I'd get up and walk over. He'd pick me up and we'd dance around the lounge, get caught up in his headphone lead. He'd lift me up into the air singing about glory days, being born in the USA and that we were dancing in the dark.

Those 46 minutes 57 seconds were some of the best, most joy-filled times of my life.

17

SMOKING ACES

0-0

The ball flew past me before I could do anything, nestling in the chain link fence with a metallic tinkle, like a wind chime. I was distracted, my attention on the crowd, scanning it for him.

0-15

Mum said he'd be here. Told him. '*Show some interest will you, these times are precious, soon he'll not want us to be there!*' she'd whispered, when she thought I wasn't paying attention

Scanning the crowd, he still wasn't here. Proud parents beaming: smiles, big eyes, cheering and pointing at their children. I felt sick. I strolled to the back of the court. Using the lip of my racket, flicked the ball up and bounced it a few times. I grasp the ball lodged in the fence, it was like plucking an apple from a tree. It wouldn't budge. But with a pull and a twist it gave. I walked to the service line, bounced the ball on the line, off the line, back on the line again. My doubles partner Joel already crouched at the net, ready to pounce on any loose return. I toss the ball. Serve. Fault. I scan the crowd again. Absence. Serve again. Fault.

0-30

He's probably busy. Doing someone else's house up, tiling, carpentry, masonry – he can do it all, I'm so proud of him; one day I hope to be just like him. Or, he might be redecorating the front room *again*. I bounce the ball, it comes back at me sharply. Catch it, lift my wrist to my forehead, dab it with my sweatband. Serve. It bounces in, a return quickly follows which I backhand down the line with interest. We trade shots. Forehand, lob, volley, lob and then Joel leaps up at the net, salmon-like. Smash.

15-30

I can't believe he didn't come. I squeeze the yellow, fuzzy ball in my hand, the pink of my nails turn white. I picture his face. Toss the ball in the air and smash the life out of it. Ace. '*Nice shot*'. Joel says, turning to celebrate the point.

30-30

First serve goes in, sets up a long rally. Each player determined not to mess up, to feel the disappointment of our families; I hope he's there somewhere. I see heads flit back and forth in my peripheral vision with each shot. Out the corner of my eye I think I see him. I return a volley. I feel stronger, emboldened, faster, more in control. They attempt a lob. I teeter back slightly, on the balls of my feet, smash a return which bounces off the tram-line, chalk puffs into the air. Turn to celebrate, think I see my dad in the crowd. Joy carving up my face like a landslide. I smile, he smiles and waves. It's not him. I turn, see Billy on the next court waving back, a proud son and a happy father.

40-30

I feel deflated, weak, I double fault. I've given up the fight. My eyes sting, could be sweat, could be tears.

40-40

I walk to the chain link fence. Bend down, shield my red eyes, pick up two errant balls. Slip one in my pocket, the other has grass on it; I pick it off, drop it to the floor, head back to the baseline. *'You can do it my boy!'* My dad's voice! My head pops up, like a dog, listening, obedient for its master's call. If I had a tail it would be wagging. I can't see him but I can smell him, the Bensons and Hedges wafting onto the court, into my nose: his distinct odour. A trail of smoke, I follow it, he's by the club house. Leaning up against the wall, watching from afar. It doesn't matter: he's here, watching me. I bounce the ball on the baseline. Toss it high into the air. The moment lasts forever as I wait for the ball to reach its optimum point in the sky. I want to impress him. I hit a powerful ace down the centre of the court. Joel turns to me. Runs back, we celebrate. *'One more like that and we win! Come on you can do it!'* takes a ball from his pocket, puts it in my hand. I want to look at my dad but I can't, I need to stay focused. Not mess up. Show him how good I've become, make him proud.

Adv – 40

I bounce the ball. Toss it in the air. Something doesn't feel right, the pressure of the shot, the situation weighing me down, my legs feel like they're made of lead. The ball hits the net – fault. Joel knocks the ball off the court. Shit. I've messed this up. *Don't look at him, don't do it*. My head stiff, neck wants to turn, to see him, but I know he'll be disappointed, I fight off the urge. I bounce the ball again - on the baseline, off the baseline, on it again. I've nothing to lose, everything to gain. I toss the ball high: it covers the sun briefly, an eclipse happening before my eyes. Then I smash it as hard and as true as I can. The fastest serve I've hit. It bounces on the line, chalk flies into the air as if the ball's smoking. Ace. Joel rushes towards me. We hug, we've won. I turn to the jubilant crowd who are jumping and shouting, celebrating with us. I peer through a gap in the crowd, see him. My heart breaks. He's missed it. He's sitting down, cigarette in his hand, reading the paper.

He was here but also somewhere else.

Like always.

18

HEAVY WEIGHT CHAMPION

This time it'll be different. I'm not going to let him win. I tell myself as my face is mashed down into the carpet. The bristles don't hurt this time: the thousands of tiny needles that used to mar my flesh don't even leave a mark nowadays. Years of abrasion at the same hands, I've grown a thick skin.

I thrash, as if in seizure. His body struggles to contain the spasms. But there's more of me now, this sapling has turned into a small tree. I feel his weight sliding on top of me, his hands grasping at my arms but he can't contain their thrashing like he used to. I break free, slide onto my side, feel him losing his control of the battle, the ongoing war. But this time I won't be a prisoner to it. This time I'll break free from his chains of bondage. I manage to wriggle onto my back. Where I wait, biding my time. Take in his heavy breathing, his sweating red face; notice the vein on his forehead become pronounced, a prominent V skittering below the surface of his greyish skin – admonishing me further, the vein a petty victory sign.

He's in full mount of me, his legs over my hips. He presses a large paw into my face, turning my face away from him, as if he doesn't want to look into the eyes of the thing that lays prostrate below him. Ashamed of this young upstart, embarrassed at how weak I am, his boy. It's as if he's gloating as he releases his grip and takes a much needed breath; his hands at his hips, happy at his torture. I spin my head back to him, watch his body rise and fall with each faltering breath he takes. We've been at this for half an hour. He's tiring, I can tell: he's not as young as he used to be. He reaches down and squishes my mouth into a pout, his fingers reek of Bensons and Hedges.

'Say it!' he bellows. Manipulating my mouth and uttering through his thin lips, a mocking, feminine voice; 'Uncle, I give up!', like a deranged ventriloquist. Any relationship that has a safe word is one to be wary of, I briefly think. But I shake my head vigorously, to disperse the thought and loosen his grasp on my mouth. I start rearing up from my hips, trying to throw him off, but he rides me like a bucking bronco, laughing and waving his arm above his head, an imaginary hat in his hand like a fucking cowboy from one of the black and white films we used to watch. 'I could do this for hours' he says, through a laugh. With one last powerful thrust he loses his balance, places a hand down to his side and it's my turn to strike, like a rattlesnake: waiting patiently for someone to step too close, become complacent. I grip his arm tight. Clamp it between both my hands, using his misbalanced distribution of weight against him. I shuffle my legs out from under his thighs, but he smothers me again like night smothers the day. But this time I'm almost up, my legs tucked beneath me, crouching. He spins around me, I hear his ragged breaths, tucks my head into his side in a headlock. 'Get out of that without moving.' he says again. His go-to line in these furious engagements. I wait. Prime myself. This time it's going to be different.

I find his belt with my hands, trace my arms around his waist slowly, like a creeping vine around a mighty oak. I don't know if my hands will make it all the way around, but I have hope and that's enough. I snuggle into him gently, trying to get my fingers to touch. All the while he continues to hold me there, stuck in his vice-like arm. He's taking a much needed break; I hear his heart pounding dully in his chest. Then I feel it, the tips of my fingers from each hand lightly stroking each other, almost there. With one final squeeze around my him I'm able to get them to lock in place, and there is no way I'm letting them go. My feet are tucked up below me, ready to release all their contained power to devastating effect. He's no clue. He's absently commenting on the television to my mother who sits watching EastEnders, whilst a heavy-weight bout plays out before her, as the underdog is about to throw the knockout punch.

I grip him tightly, my arms like pneumatic scissors, the ones firemen use to cut survivors from the wreckage of cars; my shoulder cuts into my dad's belly, like a survivor whose will to live spurs a supernatural strength. My legs fire outwards and upwards, and without knowing it, I've lifted him four feet off the floor. He's weightless as I rise to my feet, pulling him from his moorings, his arm loosens from my neck and I hear him yelp. Shock, fear, shame – who knows, but it sounds euphoric to my ears. It feels good to throw him like a ragdoll onto the sofa. I stand over him triumphantly.

'Say it.' I say but he looks on mutely, shock in his eyes. 'Say it. SAY UNCLE. Say you give up!' I glance from him to my mother; befuddlement smears her face, a blanket of confusion. When I glance back at my father, I feel... ashamed.

It's what I've always wanted: to show him that I'm not who he thinks I am. I'm a man and I can look after myself. I don't need him to rescue me anymore because I AM STRONG. And now that I've won and I've wrestled his approval of me from him, I see that I don't want it anymore. But I can't, however much I want to, put it back inside the bottle; it just won't fit back inside the fucking bottle. Something changed that day, something shifted in our relationship, and it'll never be the same again. I am no longer a boy, I am equal – and the guilt of it ate me alive. Was I just like him? Had I become the same man I'd been fighting against all these years? I just wanted to be his innocent little son again, be the boy he was proud of, even though he had a funny way of showing it. But the look in his eyes that day, fear, confusion, disappointment - things would never be the same again.

A little piece of me died that day, and it never grew back.

19

THINGS MY DAD TAUGHT ME

(WHICH I'D DO WELL TO FILTER)

1. If someone hits you, hit them back twice as hard.
2. If you get into a fight with a gang – ALWAYS hit the biggest guy first...more often than not they'll think you're a crazy bastard and leave you well alone.
3. Learn how to take a beating – if number one and two don't work.
4. Never find yourself in debt, not in money or favours.
5. Never find yourself on the social.
6. Owning your own house is the making of a man.
7. Renting is fine... but only if you must.
8. Remember your manners (he taught me this so no one would ever have to tell me to mind them).
9. Always provide for your family, by any means necessary.
10. But don't steal.

11. And don't swear.
12. Especially not at your fucking mother.
13. Nothing, NOTHING in life is free – if someone gives you something they are either crazy, a Christian or have an ulterior motive.
14. Tracy Chapman is in fact a woman, however much I would insist that *Fast Cars* sounds like it was sung by a man.
15. If someone wrongs you, you wrong'em back.
16. Life's a bitch, then you grow up and marry one (this he said with a cheeky grin that made his moustache turn up at the edges like a carnival strong guy... I assumed he was joking, I hope he was because what would that make my mother?).
17. How to snorkel, and how you needed to spit into the glass before putting it on your face.
18. How to wash out the spit before placing the mask on your face – key message there.
19. How to be strong.
20. Never *EVER* show your feelings, bury those things deep down – hide them in your guts 'til they spoil you.
21. Never show weakness.
22. If you're going to cry, do it in private: no one wants to see that.
23. Family is everything.
24. How to laugh.
25. How to make people laugh.
26. How to play a saw.
27. How to use: a saw, a hammer, and a spirit-level.
28. How to build a house.
29. How to improve a home.

30. How to swear – (this one I picked up gradually through osmosis).
31. Remember, you've never had it so easy.
32. NEVER hit a woman, there is a special place in hell for those that do this – even if she hits you first, even if she might deserve it, you *NEVER* hit a woman.
33. You can hit a transvestite if, and only if they hit you first.

In time he taught me lessons in how to be me, how to be happy with what I was, and who I wanted to be – how to love a child and have them love you back. He taught me that parenting is a strange labyrinth with no map for how to navigate it or survive it. He did the best he could and I love him to the moon and back – I just need to remember to filter what he's taught me.

20

WALLPAPERING OVER THE CRACKS

A father without a son is a sorry sight indeed. That's why I've hidden myself away, busied myself with this chore.

Since he left home I've felt lost. A captain without a crew. But after our fight he had to leave. I'm a proud man. No one, no one talks to me like that, especially my son. Unforgivable, the things he said; so I sent him packing, him and his freeloading wife. That was eight months ago now.

But I've been keeping myself busy. Playing Springsteen as loud as I want. Drinking beer in the mornings at weekends and sometimes in the week. Taken to smoking again after giving up fifteen years ago. And now I'm redecorating the house. Again. Starting afresh. Out with the old, in with the new.

· · ·

I never knew how much I'd miss him. It gets better with time they say, I think I'm suffering grief – but I can't tell anyone. Won't tell anyone.

He'll be back. I'm sure of it. Tail between his legs, licking his wounds. Wanting me to let him back in.

But it smarted. It hurt me gravely the fact that he didn't need me anymore, was above the counsel I could offer. Slinging all that shit at me. Years of pent up frustrations and hurt. He'd eventually turned on his dad, bit the hand that fed him, like a rabid dog. He seemed to forget so easily that I was the one that brought him into the world, with his mother's help of course – I'd also take him out of it if he pushed me too far, he'd known not to do that, so he fled. So, fuck him, how dare he talk to me like that in the home I've built. The sacrifices I've made, everything I've done, I've done for him; ungrateful doesn't come close. I'll remove every goddamn memory of him that lingers in this house: like a ghost, every hallway, every room, every blemish on the paintwork carries the stain of him – soon though he'll be gone. A memory that fades into noth-ingness.

He says it was my fault, that I pushed him: if you call me telling him to get up off his lazy arse and get a job, pushing him. Then yeah, I'm guilty, I guess I did shove him off the proverbial cliff. A man's got to look after his affairs: his wife, his job, his finances - he's the hunter gatherer for fuck's sake. *No son of mine relies on handouts,* I told him. He was on the social. Such shame he brought to my door. What if people found out. I'd be a laughing stock.

I don't care that he *couldn't* work, that he was on the sick. He should've known better, followed my example better. I've been sick, many times, but that didn't stop me. Kids nowadays don't know they're born - they think everything gets given to them on a bloody plate. Where's the work ethic gone? I'd turn over in my grave before I relied on handouts. Him doing that under my roof: unforgivable – brought shame on me and on the family.

What a disappointment.

I pull the scraper up over the damp wallpaper, it bunches around the head of it like icing from a piper, building gradually and then falls over my hand, like leaves falling from an autumn tree. Confetti. Blossom falling onto the wooden floorboards. Each raking thrust peeling back the years as damp paper falls to the floor in clods around me.

Stripping back the skin of this house. Revealing what's beneath, like peeling an onion. The stinging realisation of memories corrupts my eyes: I feel them swelling, misting over. Memories buried deep and painted over, rise to the surface of the murky fog of anger burning within me. I rub at my eyes with the back of a hand to stop their leaking. With another swipe of the scraper I reveal the plaster which is holding the cracks together – an internal skeleton of our life in this house. Damaged but still standing. Hurt but healed.

I pull the scraper down near the doorway. And there, in the thick paint of the door, I notice the notches: scars carved into the wood, reminding me that the past was real. Deep horizontal lacerations mar its seemingly smooth surface – hidden, painted over, erased. The wallpaper flops down, like a piece of meat carved from the old ladies' leg spinning in the kebab shop. And then I see it, a memory floods me like a tsunami – the notches, the scribbles on the wall beside it. Each one a snapshot of him, his height: we used to do it ritually on his birthday, his sister too. But he's gone. He's left me. I realise the notches stopped at his twelfth birthday. Has he been a stranger since then. Apathy. Loss. Grief at a childhood lost to this madman.

I dig the scraper into the plaster, push it deep within as if inflicting a mortal wound. I want to end this memory of him. Eradicate him from this life, from mine.

I pull the scraper up and with it the plaster cracks and I peel away any memory of him I have left. Every measurement, every reminder – flake off in dusty clumps to the floor. I feel a rage burning within me. Where it comes from, I've no idea – I want to destroy the memories of a time when I was his world and he was in my orbit, where he did what he was told. I'm not stupid. I knew he'd leave at some point, start a family of his own, fly the nest: but I wasn't ready and I don't think he is either. He'll be back I know he will.

. . .

I see his ghost now more than ever, my own personal haunting. He's in everything and everywhere he's there: hiding and waiting for me to reveal him. A phantom lurking in every corner, waiting to rub my nose in it. Ungrateful little sod.

I crumple to the floor, lie on the silt of this life, the wallpaper, the plaster, the waste products of his memories, memories I've tried so hard to erase. Then I see it, the picture he drew many years ago, when we wallpapered these halls. The childlike drawing of a boy, him, and a larger man, me. Holding hands, smiles on our faces; his writing above it, *Dad I will always love you.*

I drop the scraper. I'm alone, and I cry.

21

MR RIGHT AND MR WRONG

D ad's always right, even when he's not. He never admits it though, because that would mean he'd be wrong and as I said, he never is.

There have been times he's been forced to publicly concede defeat and it's always a messy event. Times he's found himself with nowhere else to go. When he got home he'd be furious and we'd hide in our rooms whilst he shouted at my mum, and called the 'incidental corrector' something like, a *frozen bag of urine* adding, *I wouldn't piss on him if he was on fire.*

Like a magpie jumping on something shiny, without hesitation or scrutiny, my Dad haphazardly and unscrupulously collects nuggets of information along with the told experiences of others: which he borrows, then acquires as his own. He returns these to the nest of his mind where, like a game of Chinese Whispers, his newly found treasure will undergo continual metamorphose in its repeated retelling. And there it will stay, fiercely protected and never to be called into doubt.

When I was little, for my dad to be proved wrong was like finding a needle in a haystack (and he would know because he did that once. Won a competition at a farm show, he said. Got a certificate, he said. Got loads of certificates for stuff in a drawer in the shed apparently. I've never seen them though).

His rightness has been an ever present blot in my life, a competition of sorts.

'I'm big, you're small, I'm strong, you're weak, I'm right, you're wrong.'; a mantra that I grew to believe in, knowing that whatever I did, my dad would have done it first, or at least knew something about it that I didn't.

My dad was a super hero, I looked up to him. His super-power was being the most knowledgeable man in the world; he'd agreed with me too, recounting that Stephen Hawking would run him a close second, which I thought was odd as Stephen Hawking's was in a wheelchair; even I'd outrun him, surely?

There wasn't anything Dad didn't know; he was so steadfast in his facts that he'd often get into a heated argument about something with us and anyone else who'd happen to have views or insights which differed from his.

It wasn't until I left home, flew the nest, that I began to see the chinks in the acquired knowledge he wore like an impenetrable armour.

I quickly learnt that I'd have to filter the things he'd taught me as I stepped out into the big bad world. The titbits of information that I recounted to others was nothing more but the musings of a man who made up his truths to suit his needs; fabricating his answers and chucking the truth out with the bathwater. But I like to think I'm not like him; if someone knows more, I listen; if they can educate me, then educate away. It didn't take long for me to realise that a lot of the things my dad taught me were at best, grey versions of the truth.

There is one absolute truth I am sure of though - that he loves me. And if that is the only truth I can trust then strip me of the rest.

22

A RIGHT PAIN IN THE ASS

I can count the number of times I've cried openly on one hand: properly wept, I mean. That ugly, bulldog-chewing-a-wasp face: nose streaming, eyes leaking; gut-wrenching, endless, foul sobbing.

Four times. Far too many for my liking.

Two of these I attribute to my children's births, so you could argue that both be consolidated into one finger. Technically of course, I've got a disadvantage in the finger department since the sand belt accident (didn't cry at that: should have) but for now, I'll allow two fingers for the birth of my kids. If another moment strikes, another weakness, I'll re-think the plan. No bloody way am I going to be using any more hands to count my failings. One hand's enough for anyone.

I'm pushing it now of course, this news takes me up to a

whole fistful of fingers. Five fucking times, can you believe it? I've blubbered five times. What a bloody joke.

I muse. Count each chubby finger off; just an aching reminder of how I've let myself down, the weakness out. I should keep it locked up, buried deep, hide these moments in the pit of my gut.

No one wants to see a fully grown man cry. Each finger extends, I attribute an occasion to each. Hand spread wide, fingers, well most of them, fully extended into a large palm. It's as though they are mocking me: waving at me, saying, 'Cooee, hey you! Congrats, look how weak you are...high-five!'

I want to smash my hand through the fucking wall: shatter these constant reminders, hide them away in a fibreglass cast so I don't have to look at them every day. Bloody, bastard fingers.

Eyes leaking. Wipe them. Flinch at the shameful weakness contained in those fingers.

The first time was the birth of my daughter. Holding her little head, little tufts of auburn hair, her squished face, covered in fine peach fuzz. I couldn't believe something as ugly and broken as me could have created something as beautiful and pure as this. I turned from my wife. She'd been through enough already. Didn't need to see this. My shoulders heaved, as if I were gently bouncing her to sleep. The reflection in the window gave me up instantly, a broken, sobbing mess. Her fresh eyes would never see that again; I made a promise to myself to shield her from that appalling vision that stared back at me in the glass.

The second time was my son's fault. A gorgeous little baby, came out contented and chubby. I held him: he reached out a small hand, clasped my thumb. His delicate little hand, only minutes old, barely covered my thumbnail; an instant bond. The things I'd teach him. How to wrestle, how to fight, how to play sports, how to win, how to saw, hammer, and build things; but most importantly, I'd teach him how to be a man. A daughter was great, amazing of course, but a son was even better. Special, in a way. It would ensure that a little piece of me would continue long after I was gone. He'd carry my name, carry it well, pass it on to his children, his children's children; unless he met one of those new-wave women, who'd want to emasculate him, have him change his name if they got married. I'd teach him it was wrong, women like that should be avoided at all costs. Hopefully he'd listen. Tears flowed as I imagined his future, our future, together. I dabbed them when he let my finger go, stood together looking at the great world we'd conquer together.

The third time was in a custody cell. I put that down to blood getting in my eyes rather than anything else because, at the end of the day, I'd done nothing wrong. I was right, he deserved what he got, that tight-fisted son-of-a-bitch.

. . .

The fourth time was my son's fault again. He sat in front of me, broken; drowning in debt, a husk of the boy I'd brought up. Weak, snivelling, and lost. Broke my heart. Initially I was disappointed, thought I'd taught him better: never be in debt to anyone. But we talked: turned out it was more a badly paid job, escalating rent, bills, and his daily struggle to survive, not a life of fanciful living, full of must-have gadgets that rot the brain and empty the pocket; not designer clothes, expensive holidays. He was trying to keep his head above water, support and provide for his family. The bank offered a hand, he took it. Should just have asked me. I guess he felt shame, too proud to take a hand-out – good for him, in a way. He felt he'd let me down; if I'm honest, he had. The foot was on his neck; red letters, never ending figures that would never balance. We sobbed together, I mourned for him. The loss of the man we'd created, the forfeiture of his independence, the regression into a child that needed his dad. Hugged him, the special little boy he'll always be. We cried together. Wrote him a cheque and we never spoke about it again.

The fifth time, and to complete this sorry collection, 'Cancer...' the doctor said '...prostate cancer.' His categorisation of this unseen foe gave it life, birthed something evil, which was now festering deep within me. 'You're very lucky, we've caught it early, and you should make a full recovery!', he uttered through a rehearsed smile.

Key word here, *should*. Nothing I could do. Shock. Mind

racing. No words to say. He leaves. Gives me a minute to pull myself together. I'm alone. Lost. Cry. Something breaks within me, I heave, and nothing comes. Tears stream down my face, dapple my jeans. He returns, hands me a leaflet.

I sit.

Let the tears flow.

23

RECONCILIATION

I *miss you.*

Three words.

That's all he sent me.

Three words that are supposed to undo a lifetime of hurt and anguish at his hands, as if those three words are a magic eraser that'll make everything just go away.

The pub's quiet, which is good. His message has put me slightly off kilter, as if the ground is being pulled out from under me. Seeing Dad flash up on my phone brought back all my childhood angst in one raging tsunami of emotions.

. . .

I miss you.

Is it wrong to wish I never heard from him again? The last time we spoke, well, argued, he'd hit me. I still remember the solid crack as his opened palm hit me, as if someone had just broken a dead branch over their knee. I should be grateful he hit me with an open palm: at least he showed some restraint. I remember his hate filled eyes staring back at me; I wasn't his little boy anymore. Then I watched as his eyes melted into blue pools of regret – you can't put this back in the bottle however much you try. He's lucky my wife was there, I'd have gone for him. She pulled me away to the safety of our room, where we packed and left. He just sat in the dining room, his eyes fixed to the floor: never looked up as we trampled down the stairs with what we could carry and left, never to come back. My mother pleaded with us to stay, *'you know what your father's like once he's had a drink,'* as if she were trying to excuse his behaviour. It was in that moment that I felt pity for her, and for the first time I could see that she'd defend him to the end of the world, like she had done all our lives: whatever the cost.

I take a sip from my beer. It's cold and makes me shudder. I glance down at my phone on the table, swipe it open.

I miss you.

. . .

Those three fucking words again. Was it some form of a veiled apology? Testing the water? What the hell does he want me to reply? Was he drunk, again? I pick up my phone, tap in my response.

Good. And you're never going to get to see your grand-children...

My finger hovers over send. But I delete it: watch the characters fall away one at a time and I'm left with a blinking line, waiting for me to type. I take another sip of beer, try to compose myself, but all I can think about is wanting to hurt him, hurt him like he had me. But I wasn't going to use my children as bait: that was callous, something he'd do. He'd use me and my sister as pawns in his own battles and would sacrifice us in the blink of an eye if it meant he got what he wanted at the end of it. Much like how he played chess, always thinking three steps ahead, ready to sacrifice his pawns if it meant he could win.

My wife would want me to make amends, be the bigger man, show him that I'm nothing like him, and she's right. I *should* be the bigger man, be an example to my children. Just because I'm his son doesn't make me a doormat. My children should see that forgiveness is a tangible concept, something that can really change things. I should be a role model to them, show them that however hurt they've been, that forgiving someone, even a monster, is one of the most powerful things they could ever do. There is healing in the words. There is the opportunity to lay down all that baggage and be free from its suffocating embrace. I know what to do but it doesn't make it any easier. I pick up the phone, my hands trembling, like they used to do when I was a child living under his tyrannical rule.

I miss you.

What do I write? The blinking line taunts me, raises my anxiety. My hands tremble uncontrollably. What do I say in response to those three small words? I sit still for a moment: drinking in the atmosphere, the smell of the pub, the beating of my heart, the speed at which I'm breathing – everything dialled up to ten. My fingers are tapping. I can't seem to stop them.

I miss you too.

Four small words, but it's all I can manage. Anything more would be a lie; because if I'm honest with myself, however much I wish it wasn't true, however much I try to hide it, I do miss him, and my children should get to see their grandparents. I send the message. Drink my beer with a shaking hand. I glance down at my phone on the table, the conversation in grey and green speech bubbles.

I miss you.

.   .   .

I miss you too.

And there below my message I see three dots.

...

Shit, he's replying. He must have been waiting by his phone. I sit there, willing a response to come, but dreading what might be said. I finish my beer and return my eyes to the phone. Nothing; the three dots continue blinking. It's been five minutes. I go to leave; the phone vibrates on the table.

I think about you every day. About what happened. I'm sorry.

I can't stop the tears. Something that was broken deep within me feels fixed for the first time in years, as if someone turned off a tap that was leaking toxic waste into my soul, polluting me from the inside out. *I'm sorry*; two small words, but ones I've never heard uttered from his mouth. I pick up the phone. Wipe my eyes with the back of a hand. Start dialling.

24

THINGS I WANT TO TEACH MY DAUGHTERS

(FILTERED)

1. If someone hits you, don't hit them back (*I've learnt this the hard way*).
2. If someone pulls a knife or a weapon on you, run. There's nothing wrong in trying to preserve your life and risk looking like a coward in the process.
3. If someone you know, a friend, offers you drugs: decline but always be there for them, they'll need you when the time is right.
4. If you get lost, ask for directions; there is no shame in not knowing where you are going.
5. Get lost in a book from time-to-time, too.
6. Be kind to those around you, everyone is fighting a battle you can't see. So be kind, above all else.
7. There is nothing you could do that would make me love you any less.
8. If you have problems, talk about them.
9. If you don't want to talk to me about them, then talk to your mum or your sister.
10. If a boyfriend or husband hits you, talk to your father

about it: then check with your mother that your father's course of action is appropriate – I'm only human and you're the most precious things in the world to me.

11. Never EVER feel like you can't come home – the door will always be open for you.

12. Don't be like your father – learn about cars so you'll never be taken for a ride. Some mechanics and salesmen can't deal with a woman that knows about cars.

13. Don't be like your father – learn to curb that anger.

14. No one owns you.

15. No one owns what you will become.

16. If you are struggling, we will do all we can to help you.

17. Never be afraid to ask.

18. There is no shame in being on benefits, if you need them, use them – that's what they are there for.

19. That said, always remember what you're capable of and what you can achieve when you put your mind to it. You can bring something to the world no one else can.

20. Green Day, David Bowie, John Denver and Fleetwood Mac are the pinnacle of good music.

21. Be what you want to be, whatever that is – if you want to sell burgers in McDonald's for the rest of your life, if that makes you happy, then that's okay in my book.

22. Remember the good times.

23. Forget about the bad times, but learn what you can from them first.

24. Find the one that makes your heart sing, don't be swayed by riches or looks – find the one that completes you: the one you can laugh with, cry with and be *you* with.

25. Don't sacrifice your beautiful selves for the approval of others – be you, there is only one of you and you are enough just as you are.

26. Care for those in need.

27. Help those who are struggling, even if it means you go without.

28. Surround yourself with true friends, not acquaintances.

29. Be supportive of your sister – be there when she needs you.

30. Claim your mistakes and own them. They are what shape you. If you've done something wrong, admit it and move on – these refinements build character.

31. Remember that your mother and father are sometimes wrong – *sometimes*.

32. As long as you try, you're a winner in my book.

33. Don't become a mobile phone zombie – if you're in company, put the mobile phone away. Nothing is more valuable than real, face-to-face relationships.

34. Break the mould; be weird, be fierce, be who you want to be.

35. Eat healthily.

36. Look after your body, you only get one of them.

37. Tracy Chapman, the singer of 'Fast Car', is a woman.

38. Love whomever you choose: don't be swayed by opinion, unless that is from your mother and father. We know best, but as I said, sometimes, *sometimes* we get it wrong.

39. Develop a good sense of humour: people say sarcasm is the lowest form of wit, but in our book, it's hilarious. So, be sarcastic if you want, just don't be a dick about it.

40. Dance, sing, laugh, cry and love unashamedly.

41. When you have children, remember that childhood disappears in the blinking of an eye. Love your children as if there is no tomorrow, tell them that you love them often, cuddle them so they'll feel it for the rest of the week.

42. If someone invites you to their home, take something to offer them for their hospitality.

43. Play games.

44. Lose games.

45. Competitiveness is healthy no matter what your mother says: especially in games, otherwise they wouldn't have made winners and losers.

46. If you lose, remember you are the best loser.

47. So be gracious in defeat.

48. Fail at things: it builds character.

49. Trust your gut: if it doesn't feel right, then it's probably not.

50. When you're older, come visit your parents from time-to-time – we love you and will always love you.

51. When you visit us, bring cake or biscuits or chocolate. Or alcohol.

52. Just because we do things one way, doesn't mean it's the right way.

Girls, I hope some of this is useful to you. Some of these things I learned from my father; some I have had to filter through my own learned wisdom and experiences; some are tried and tested and some are new additions. Be the filter for your children: add to these things, develop them and hone them to your own code. I love you. Never, ever forget that. You are my world and I am so happy for the love you show me – you make me proud each and every day. I hope that one day you'll be able to see that.

One final thing, never ever allow yourself to get too hungry – if you're anything like your father you'll become *hangry* and there is nothing more troublesome than a *hangry* person. Believe me.

CRASH BANG WALLOP

The roads are icy, a million stars reflect back at my headlights from the frost covered road, a galactic highway leading me on. I reach over to the fans and turn them up. The instant heat bringing small but much needed relief. I clutch the steering wheel which feels slippery under my hands, condensation making them slick against the plastic. I hold my right hand out over the heater; feel my skin thaw my bones, becoming unstuck as the ligaments defrost.

The windscreen is misting so I reach down and click all the various buttons on the dash, trying to head off this blinding mist creeping across the screen; the fans whir into life, causing me to make my eyes into slits whilst I'm blasted from every angle. My wife usually controls the visibility in the car, I should learn which buttons do what, but to me, it's just a car, gets me from A to B, so learning about which buttons de-mist the windscreen are low on my list of priorities. Without her here, I wish I'd paid attention.

. . .

A circle of clear windscreen starts to reappear, slowly spreading across the glass. I keep my speed and head into the darkness, with the white dashes of the road guiding me into towards my destination. Home.

I stop at a junction. Have to lower the windows on either side of the car to see if there are any oncoming vehicles. I press the buttons on the door and brace myself against the sudden cutting breeze that slaps me across the face, the roads are empty so I pull out, turn left towards home. I'll be there in thirty-five minutes, but with each moment that passes between here and there my mind races as fast as my heart. The closer I get to home, the closer I get to seeing him, my father, and to opening old wounds.

The last time I saw him, he'd hit me. Hard across the face. That's why I'm doing this alone, unsure of what awaits me when I get there, and there is no way I'm exposing my children to the hostile, toxic environment that stripped me of my childhood. I've given promises and reassurances to my wife that I won't do anything silly, that I won't throttle the bastard, and she'd seemed happy with that. But the closer I get, the more I keep thinking about putting my hands around his throat and squeezing. It'd be therapy surely, some type of Freudian, cathartic release; but thinking about it, it'd just be patricide.

I check the rear-view mirror and see a car behind me. It's a good way away, but its lights are on full-beam: those LED lights that are so bright they can bring on a migraine. The screen and the windows are clearing now, it's only taken me three hours to work out how to get some semblance of safety. But it's boiling and I'm sweating and with no lights down these country roads, except for the car behind me, I dare not turn the heating down or I'll be plunged back into fog.

My phone starts to ring. It's on the dashboard in one of those plastic contraptions that help you be hands-free but only serve to help take your eyes off the road as you fiddle with trying to answer the damn thing. I glance at the screen. Dad. I take my left hand off the wheel, press the breaks slightly as I go into a bend. Tap the screen. Nothing. I come out of the bend, the phone's still ringing. I tap again. Furiously tapping without looking and then I hear his voice.

'Hello?'

'Hi Dad, everything okay, I'm driving?'

'Yeah I was just calling to get your ETA, whereabouts are you?'

'Just coming through the lanes.'

· · ·

'Right. So you'll be...'

'About half an hour.' We both say in unison. And we both laugh. The car behind me has caught up as I've realised that I've taken my foot off the accelerator and slowed to negotiate the winding roads. It's right on top of me now, bright white lights illuminating me through the rear window. I lift a hand up: click the switch on the rear-view mirror taking the glare out of my eyes.

'Mum's got some dinner on.'

'Dad I'd said I'd already eaten, I don't...'

'Oh, well she thought it would be nice for us to chat over dinner. But that's fine, I guess we'll just...'

'It's okay, I'll eat it, it'll be nice.' I don't want to get this meeting off on the wrong foot, so I hand him an olive branch.

'Oh that's brilliant, your mother will be pleased.'

The car behind me swerves out to pass but retreats as we enter another bend. He starts flashing his lights; each one making me blink, momentarily blinding me. I remember something from my childhood, extend the olive branch again.

'Could do with one of your golf balls about now,' I offer into the car.

'One of my what?'

'Golf balls, you remember? You used to keep them in the glovebox...'

He's silent for a moment, coughs, clearing his throat. 'I remember now. That seems like a lifetime ago, I was a different man back then. You still remember that?'

'Of course I do.' It traumatised me, is what I want to say, but don't. 'You had a stash of them reserved for right about now. Bloody can't see a thing with his headlights... you'd have dropped a few out already, I'm sure of it. Taught him a lesson a few miles back.'

'Yeah, that was a different time.'

His voice sounds little, like he's ashamed. The car behind me cuts out into the other lane as we approach a bend. Hits the accelerator. There are lights coming from up ahead, he doesn't see them. He draws alongside me, beeping his horn.

'Is everything okay?' I hear my dad ask. I remain silent as the car swerves towards me, our wing mirrors almost touching, aware of the oncoming vehicle. I hit the brakes, see fleetingly the driver waving his hand at me, then realise he's flipping me the finger; within seconds he's in front of me, pulled in sharply, almost loses his back end as the car in the other lane flashes by, narrowly missing each other as it passes.

'Sorry Dad, yeah. Everything's okay, was just concentrating. Right, I better go now, I'll be there in twenty.' The car in front speeds off into the night, his red lights like a demon's eyes retreating into the distance.

'Good, good. We'll see you when you get here.' His voice full of hope.

'Okay Dad, have the dinner on the table.'

I turn a sharp corner in the road.

'Love you, son.'

. . .

It hangs there for a moment, what he's said. I don't know what to say. I've not said it back since we started talking again, sometimes that word can just be a reaction, you say it back out of habit. But when I next say those words to him I want to mean it, not just placate him. Something large wanders out from the bushes, a badger. I swerve to miss it. The car lurches, I try to get back in control, feel the back end of the car lose traction and spin out into the other side of the road, hear the screech of tyres, feel the passenger side lifting, then I'm tipping, flipping, airborne.

A thousand and one things run through my mind, but I utter only one.

'Dad!'

TETHERED

(ORIGINALLY PUBLISHED IN ELLIPSIS ZINE)

I sit here. Contemplating the next steps. I voice my concerns, to everyone and no one; discuss the ways we can get past this, how he could have been so stupid, why he never listened to me, why he had to do what he did. But through all my discussions, I keep coming up short of a definitive answer or reason.

You should have listened to me, I yell at him.

But my son remains mute. Something I'm slowly coming to terms with.

Black wires tether him to the bed, ensnaring him within a web of cables. A dolphin trapped in a fisherman's net: suspended, imprisoned with glassy eyes, his tongue lolling from his mouth. Turning from life to death; a machine anchoring his body to the bed, ensuring he doesn't just float away into the abyss. It breathes for him, feeding him oxygen in a whirling mechanical tide. The storms rage but the contraption keeps him alive - if you can call this amalgamation of wires and flesh, life.

Lights blink intermittently, combinations of green and red: like watching a fairground ride on mute.

Would you believe, I've forgotten what he sounds like: such an odd concept to grasp. I never knew the last time we spoke, the last argument, when I heard him say he loved me... I had no idea it was going to be the last. If I had known, I would have paid more attention. I would have burned his sweet voice into my mind, branded myself with it. I wish I'd paid him more attention whilst he was here, instead of the immeasurable time I spend with him now... there.

He still talks to me. Silently, of course. It's now an abhorrent consolidation of contorted and strained facial tics, and the occasional fit, where his limbs flap around like a bird having a heart attack; the throws of death descending over him like a vengeful fringe, tickling his body, stirring it into motion with its tendrils of temptation - calling him to the place beyond, away from me. These unseen sirens of the underworld stir his brain into life. His body fidgets, the lights flash, his heart rate spikes, then nothing: just the mechanical lung, expanding and depressing, driving air into his forlorn body.

Is it wrong to wish the passing of your son?

Or am I a monster?

I just pray that death would stop teasing him.

That instead, it would just reach out its hands and drag him away in its undertow, clasp his soul and pull it free of this fleshy prison. The hope I clung to has slowly been replaced with the aching pain of despair.

He is a shell of the boy I knew. Of the confident man he became.

He's a husk of the life he was.

For a moment he looks at peace, as if he's been liberated from his half-grave. But the machine inflates his chest again and the others resume their methodical beeping and whooshing.

I reach out a shaking hand. Tap him on the nose. Say bonk one last time.

Lay hold of the cables tethering him to the wall socket.

Anchoring him to the bed and his perpetual prison.

And I pull.

ACKNOWLEDGMENTS

Firstly I would like to say this book wouldn't exist if it wasn't for my own father, so this book is for you, Dad.

I would also like to thank Meg Pokrass and Jude Higgins - for without attending your workshop on the Novella-in-Flash at the Bath Flash Fiction Festival, these stories would still only be memories. Thank you for your tireless dedication to the craft of Flash, and for inspiring writers to create.

To all those authors who have read Tethered and contributed words of praise - thank you. You will never know how much it means to have you be a part of this book.

Adam Lock - my beta reader, friend and editor of a few of these stories, thank you. You are a true gentleman and a fabulous writer and advocate of the indie author scene. Keep fighting the good fight.

To the magazines where a few of these stories have

appeared, thank you for giving a platform for writers to be heard.

To my good friends Tony and Tomek - thank you for always believing in me.

To you the reader, thank you for picking up this book and for reading it: I hope that you've enjoyed it. I also hope that these stories help: that they might show you that you are not alone, that you can survive, that there is still hope. I hope there may be healing in these words, and a message that says it's okay to be scarred and damaged. If you've read these stories and they have struck a nerve and you need to talk to someone, please, please find someone to talk to. Don't bottle it up. Speak your truth to someone who will listen.

To my amazing wife Anna - thank you for your never ending encouragement and for challenging me to write these stories when I thought about giving up.

To my daughters Eva and Sophie - just remember that Daddy tried to be the best daddy he could be, but sometimes I may have got it wrong. And I will do so again, no doubt. But for you, I endeavour to keep trying to be better.

And lastly thank you to God and his many blessings on my life.

Me and the boy.

Image by Valaya Salter

ABOUT THE AUTHOR

Ross Jeffery is the author of Juniper. A Bristol based writer and Executive Director of Books for STORGY Magazine. Ross has been published in print with The Writing Collective, STORGY Books, Ellipsis Zine, The Bath Flash Fiction Festival, Project 13 Dark and Shlock Magazine. His work has also appeared in various online journals such as STORGY Magazine, About Magazine TX, Elephants Never, 101 Fiction, Ellipsis Zine, Soft Cartel and Idle Ink. Ross lives in Bristol with his wife (Anna) and two children (Eva and Sophie).

ALSO BY ROSS JEFFERY

ROSS JEFFERY HAS BIRTHED THE LOVECHILD OF
STEPHEN KING AND CORMAC MCCARTHY.'
- PRIYA SHARMA -

JUNIPER
BY ROSS JEFFERY

Available from Amazon
In eBook, Paperback & Hardback

'Tome is equal parts Shawshank Redemption and H. P. Lovecraft, a masterstroke of Gothic horror.'

- JOSEPH SALE -

TOME
ROSS JEFFERY

Available Winter 2020

Book Two of the Juniper Trilogy

Printed in Great Britain
by Amazon